Making the Best Man's Speech

John Bowden
2nd edition

Every effort has been made to identify and acknowledge the sources
of the material quoted throughout this book. The author and
publishers apologise for any errors or omissions, and would be
grateful to be notified of any corrections that should appear in any
reprint or new edition.

Published in 1999 by
How To Books Ltd, 3 Newtec Place,
Magdalen Road, Oxford OX4 1RE, United Kingdom
Tel: (01865) 793806   Fax: (01865) 248780
info@howtobooks.co.uk
www.howtobooks.co.uk

First edition 1999
Second edition 2000
Reprinted 2001
Reprinted 2002
Reprinted 2003 (twice)

British Library Cataloguing in Publication Data.
A catalogue record for this book is available from
the British Library.

Cover design by Baseline Arts Ltd, Oxford
Produced for How To Books by Deer Park Productions
Typeset by Anneset, Weston-super-Mare
Printed and bound in Great Britain

NOTE: The material contained in this book is set out in good faith for
general guidance and no liability can be accepted for loss or expense
incurred as a result of relying in particular circumstances on
statements made in the book. Laws and regulations are complex and
liable to change, and readers should check the current position with
the relevant authorities before making personal arrangements.

Contents

Preface

So you have been asked 'to say a few words' on the big day. The problem is we don't get much practice, do we? That's why this little handbook will prove so useful to you. Quite simply, it will show you how to prepare and present a unique and memorable best man's speech that even the most seasoned public speaker would be proud of.

There are a number of old things which we are well rid of – shell suits, London smog, the Berlin Wall – but there are still other things that we would be foolish to let slip away. The traditional British best man's speech is one of them. Whether you feel honoured or lumbered – or both – if you get back to basics, concentrate on the essentials, and learn about the things that really matter, your speech will sparkle like vintage champagne!

John Bowden

For Gordon, who did the business at my
wedding ... but I forgive him!

1 Learning the Essentials

Stand up to be seen; speak up to be heard; shut up to be appreciated.

5 things that really matter

1 **CONFIRMING THE PROGRAMME**

2 **KNOWING YOUR PURPOSE**

3 **MAKING HAPPY TALK**

4 **KEEPING THE AUDIENCE INTERESTED**

5 **REMEMBERING THE GOLDEN RULES**

Recipe for a successful best man's speech? No waffle and plenty of shortening. The ingredients required are humour and optimism, all applied with liberal helpings of praise.

Think of your speech as a gourmet meal. Your opening lines should serve up a tasty little starter that really whets the audience's appetite for a memorable main course. Your closing words should provide a delectable dessert with a delicious aftertaste.

What you must do is prepare and deliver a relevant, upbeat, jokey little speech, which includes plenty of compliments and tributes to the happy couple and keeps *everyone present* amused and entertained.

The audience is on your side. They are willing you to do well and, quite frankly, they won't give a damn if you fluff a line or two. What they *will* mind, though, is if it becomes embarrassingly obvious that you have not even bothered to take the time or effort to find out what is expected of you.

IS THIS YOU?

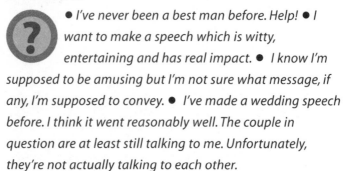

● I've never been a best man before. Help! ● I want to make a speech which is witty, entertaining and has real impact. ● I know I'm supposed to be amusing but I'm not sure what message, if any, I'm supposed to convey. ● I've made a wedding speech before. I think it went reasonably well. The couple in question are at least still talking to me. Unfortunately, they're not actually talking to each other.

● What I really need is a simple checklist of do's and don'ts for a best man's speech.

① CONFIRMING THE PROGRAMME

Traditionally, the **bride's father** speaks first. He needs to come across as solid, thoughtful and sensible. But he also needs to allow the lighter, more humorous side of his personality to shine through.

Next comes the **bridegroom** whose contribution is expected to be a little more varied and adventurous. He has to show the guests that he understands the importance and significance of the occassion, yet he needs to be quite amusing too.

Finally, comes the **best man.** In footballing terms, you are the sports journalist who has just witnessed the transfer of a star player – the blushing bride. Whilst the first two speakers can be compared to club managers who are personally involved, you can be more objective and share a little gossip and chit chat with the gathered supporters. Your speech should contain plenty of humour and friendly digs at the bridegroom – but it should be underpinned with an equal number of congratulatory thoughts and optimistic remarks.

However, this conventional pattern of wedding speeches assumes that the bride was brought up by two parents – and today over two million people in Britain haven't been. And things have changed socially and culturally too. Girl power and all that. Today far more women than ever literally want to speak for themselves.

So now it's perfectly acceptable for speeches to be made by other people instead of, or as well as, the traditional big three – perhaps by a **close family friend**, by the **bride's mother**, by the **bride and groom jointly**, or by the **bride** herself. It all depends on the particular circumstances, attitudes and backgrounds of the newlyweds.

The speeches usually begin after the guests have finished eating. Make sure their glasses are charged *before* anyone speaks. If there is a toastmaster, he will say something like 'Ladies and Gentlemen, pray silence for Mr Ben Nevis who will propose a toast to Mr Sydney and Mrs Pearl Harbour.' If there is no toastmaster, the best man should do the honours, but in a less formal manner: 'Ladies and Gentlemen, please be silent as Mr Ben Nevis proposes a toast to Mr Sydney and Mrs Pearl Harbour.'

The important thing is to find out what the programme of speeches will be and precisely where you will fit into it.

 KNOWING YOUR PURPOSE

The main purpose of every wedding speech is to propose a toast or to respond to one, or to do both.

- **The bride's father (or close family friend, relative or godfather)**: proposes a toast to the bride and groom.
- **The bridegroom (possibly with the bride)**: responds to the toast and then proposes a second toast.

- **The best man (or best girl)**: responds to the second toast on behalf of the bridesmaids (and any other attendants).

A simple acknowledgement of your purpose within the first few sentences of your speech is all that is required: 'It seems strange replying to the toast to the bridesmaids because, as you can see, I'm not a bridesmaid . . .'

 MAKING HAPPY TALK

This is a happy day. Your speech should be:

- **Optimistic**: this is not the time to share your personal woes, paint a gloomy picture of the present or offer dire predictions about the future.
- **Enlivened with humour**: the bride's father and her new hubby have probably already done more than enough of the serious and emotional stuff. What the audience wants now is to relax, sit back and have a good laugh.
- **A tribute to the happy couple**: even though your offering should be sprinkled with insults, they should all be friendly and liberally sugared with praise.

 KEEPING THE AUDIENCE INTERESTED

Your aim is to **communicate** with your audience – to establish a dialogue with them – to turn listeners into participants. How? By involving them. By allowing them not only to hear your speech but also to **experience** it.

Nowadays, the average audience has the attention span of a two-year-old. People have been programmed to absorb soundbites. Talk at length about people or places they don't know and they will soon lose interest.

As you plan and prepare your speech, remember these three little words: **KISS THE BRIDE**

This will remind you of two vital things. First, the word **KISS** will remind you to:

Keep

It

Short and

Simple

In the Bible, the story of the Creation is told in 400 words (that's under 3 minutes) and the Ten Commandments are covered in less than 300. Try to say everything you need to say in less than 1,000 words (7 minutes). Size *does* matter. And no speech can be entirely bad if it's short enough.

As the mother whale said to her young: 'Remember, my dears, you can only be harpooned while you're spouting. So don't go spouting on and on.'

Secondly, the words **THE BRIDE** will remind you that it is *her* big day. Don't spoil it by embarrassing her or by knocking the institution of marriage.

 REMEMBERING THE GOLDEN RULES

This simple ten-point plan will ensure the contents of your speech will not be cited as grounds for divorce:

- Thank the bridegroom for his toast to the bridesmaids.
- Add a few complimentary comments of your own.
- Offer some sincere and optimistic thoughts about the bride, the groom and the marriage.
- Include a few friendly digs at the bridegroom.
- A little innuendo is fine but avoid anything really smutty:

Something old, something new, plenty borrowed, nothing blue!

- Congratulate the bridegroom on his good luck and wish the couple happiness in the future.

- Learn your opening and closing lines by heart (but rehearse the rest of your speech) not to be perfect, but to be comfortable. If you feel comfortable, so will the audience.

- Try to wrap it up in no more than seven minutes. Leave them wanting more.

- Relax and have fun!

- Read the tele-messages (having first checked that they are suitable for public consumption).

MAKING WHAT MATTERS WORK FOR YOU

✓   Make sure you know the order of speeches.

✓   Don't forget to respond to that toast.

✓   Keep the overall tone light and upbeat.

✓   Your speech must be interesting – even to people who have not met all the characters you are talking about.

✓   Follow the ten golden rules and you won't go far wrong.

2 Saying it with Humour

People expect a best man's speech to include plenty of humour.

4

things that really matter

1 MAKING 'EM LAUGH

2 HAVING A FRIENDLY DIG AT THE BRIDEGROOM

3 TELLING JOKES AND STORIES

4 REHEARSING A FEW 'AD-LIB' LINES

When it comes to questions of taste and taboos, propriety and political correctness, things continually change. You have to keep up with the times. You must use your own judgement and common sense about the question and perhaps take advice from the bride and groom.

Know your audience. Judge how broadminded they are likely to be. If you have any doubts about a joke, cut it. It may be a stunningly good wheeze in your opinion, but if you offend or embarrass your audience, you will have a very hard time winning them over again.

The important thing to remember is that a wedding is a **family** occasion. Any speech which aims at the lowest common denominator will not inspire affection or respect, and such a performance is ultimately barren of genuine humour.

IS THIS YOU?

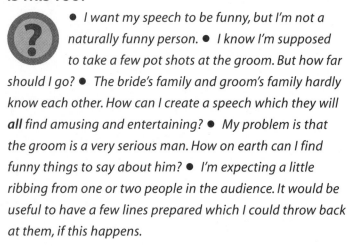

● *I want my speech to be funny, but I'm not a naturally funny person.* ● *I know I'm supposed to take a few pot shots at the groom. But how far should I go?* ● *The bride's family and groom's family hardly know each other. How can I create a speech which they will* ***all*** *find amusing and entertaining?* ● *My problem is that the groom is a very serious man. How on earth can I find funny things to say about him?* ● *I'm expecting a little ribbing from one or two people in the audience. It would be useful to have a few lines prepared which I could throw back at them, if this happens.*

 ## MAKING 'EM LAUGH

Everyone loves a good gag. If you can find a *relevant* joke you are onto a winner. It will relax the audience and you. Matching your choice of material to the nature of the guests is easy when the group all know each other - and they all know the bride and groom. At wedding receptions this is often *not* the case, so you must choose your jokes and one-liners with care.

*Tell uncomplicated jokes and stories that **everyone** present will find interesting and amusing.*

Let's assume that only half the crowd knows that the bridegroom, Dave is into karaoke. There is no need to bore the other half by singing his praises. One simple gag will do the job:

'Even though his public fail to appreciate it, Dave has a very tuneful voice and when he sings his head off on Karaoke Night, it really improves his appearance.'

Now **everyone** present should find that amusing - with the possible exception of Dave.

Vary your style and pace. Include a few snappy one-liners together with one or two longer and slower jokes or stories.

Remember to keep your speech clean – well clean*ish* anyway. Nobody will be shocked by a little innuendo - in fact, that's expected:

'Like another couple I know - a very unfortunate match. They're both Welsh, but she's a Presbyterian and he's Sunday opening. . .'

'In a few moments the happy couple will be going upstairs to put their things together.'

'Did you hear about the couple who couldn't tell the difference between vaseline and putty? A week later their windows fell out . . . which was the least of their problems.'

You'll find plenty more potential material in Chapter 7. However, before you tell a story or crack a joke, ask yourself whether it passes this test which Bob Monkhouse devised for all his potential material:

1. Do *you* think it is funny?
2. Can you say it confidently and with comfort?
3. Is there any danger of offending anyone?
4. Will they understand and appreciate it?

Do *you* think it is funny?
If you're not really happy about a joke or a story you will not

tell it well. Not only that, the guests probably won't find it funny either. Follow this showbiz adage: If in doubt, leave it out.

Can you say it confidently and with comfort?

Before you spin a yarn, ask yourself: Is this story right for *me*? A true story about one of your own amusing or embarrassing experiences will have far more effect and novelty value than a repeated old chestnut which some of your audience may have heard before.

Is there any danger of offending anyone?

The traditional advice is to avoid anything racist, sexist or ageist, and steer well clear of politics, religion and disabilities. The problem is that if you do this, many of the best topics for jokes are automatically excluded from your speech. So use your common sense. Uncle Jack, in his electric wheelchair, would prefer to have his leg pulled about the fine he incurred for speeding to get to the wedding on time, than to be ignored altogether.

Will they understand and appreciate it?

Your audience may be aged anything between 2 and 92 (nowadays even older) and they will probably have a wide range of backgrounds. So it is impossible to give a speech totally suited to everyone. However, what you can do is avoid extremes of, on the one hand, telling childish jokes and, on the other hand, telling complicated, technical stories, comprehensible only to a professor of nuclear physics.

If the guests don't laugh at your jokes and stories, it really isn't their fault – it's yours!

② HAVING A FRIENDLY DIG AT THE BRIDEGROOM

It is traditional for the best man to have a bit of a go at the bridegroom. Don't say anything nasty or vindictive, though. All that is required is a little mild, friendly, humorous banter.

For a gag to work, people need to know what you're talking about.

Your audience will only laugh at a parody of what it *recognises* as the groom's little foibles. So think about his looks, characteristics, job and hobbies. There is bound to be plenty of scope for humour here.

The guests must recognise that while all your jokes are clearly exaggerations, they are nonetheless based on fundamental truths about the groom. For instance, there is no point in laughing at his colourful use of language, unless you are sure the audience knows he spends most of his waking hours effing and blinding, and is not merely the kind who just might bleat out an apologetic 'oh, blast' - and then only if mauled by a lion.

Say he is not known for his sartorial elegance, then you might observe that:

'Doesn't (*bridegroom*) look wonderful? They made great suits in the 1980's.'

If he's known to be a bit of a boozer:

'(*Bride*), I've got some important news for you: (*Bridegroom*) just told me he's not going to drink anymore. Unfortunately, he's not going to drink any less either.'

If he's a legal eagle:

'I dream't that (*bridegroom*) died and went to the gates of heaven where he was interviewed by St Peter to see if he should be let into heaven or hell. "I don't know why I died so young," complained (*bridegroom*), "It doesnt seem fair, I'm only (*age*)." "I know," replied St Peter, "but according to all the time you've billed your clients for, you're at least 502." '

If he's really into music:

'(*Bridegroom*) has a magnificent CD collection. One day he went into a record shop and asked for *Rhapsody in Blue*, but the girl said they hadn't got it. "Well would you mind taking another look?" he asked. "Perhaps they do it in some other colour."'

A neat little trick is to go one stage further and to damn him through faint praise. The idea here is to issue a half-hearted compliment which really does no more that highlight your poor victim's mediocrity:

'(*Bridegroom's*) speech was both good and original; but the part that was good was not original, and the part that was original was not good.'

'(*Bridegroom*) is a man who only comes along once in a lifetime . . . I'm only sorry it had to be during *my* lifetime!'

'This man is an inspiration to us all. Let's face it, if he can make it, then anyone can.'

 TELLING JOKES AND STORIES

The key word here is *telling*. There is a fundamental difference in written and spoken humour. To illustrate this let's consider how a story can improve in the telling over the bald facts on the printed page.

Suppose you want to tell the guests about your and the bridegroom's drinking habits. Use the fact that you are on your feet to your advantage. Begin with a couple of general one-line gags about boozing to get the laughs flowing, before relating a story which you can act out. For example, you might say:

'Do you know, in this town there are more than 350 pubs. But I can tell you that (*bridegroom*) and I haven't been in one of them. Problem is we can never remember which one of them we haven't been in.

We drank so much on our trip to Europe last summer that when we got to Italy we were the only ones in the party who couldn't see anything wrong with the Tower of Pisa. And we were so drunk when we came back, that they had to pay duty on us to get us through Customs. We don't just drink to excess . . . we drink to anything.

But things are going to change - for (*bridegroom*) anyway. She who must be obeyed has decreed it. Last week (*bride*) found a case of whisky hidden in the kitchen of their new house and told (*bridegroom*) to empty each and every bottle down the sink, or else . . . so last Saturday, after the football, he and I reluctantly proceeded with the unhappy task.

(*Bridegroom*) drew the cork from the first bottle and poured the contents down the sink, with the exception of a couple of glasses, which we drank.

Then I pulled the cork from a second bottle and did likewise, with the exception of another two glasses, which we consumed.

He emptied the third bottle, except for two glasses, which we drank and then took the cork from the fourth sink, poured the glass down the bottle and drank that too.

I pulled the bottle from the next glass, we drank two sinks

out of it, and emptied the rest down the cork.

Then he pulled the sink from the next bottle and poured it down the glass and we drank the cork, and finally I took the glass from the last bottle, emptied the cork, poured the sink down the rest and drank the pour.

When we had emptied everything, (*bridegroom*) steadied the house with one hand, counted the bottles and glasses and corks with the other and found there were 31.

To make sure, I recounted them when they came by again and this time there were 72.

As the house came around the next time, we counted them again, and finally we had all the houses and sinks and glasses and corks and bottles counted, except one house, which we then drank.'

Obviously the humour would be greatly enhanced if you acted out the story and included a few relevant movements, gestures, expressions, slurs and stumbles as you both become more and more inebriated.

The precise wording and style of delivery of a joke or story, of course, is *yours*, not mine. But I hope this simple example will encourage the novice to look at his material a little more carefully to see what can be extracted over and above the obvious punchline reaction. We'll return to this subject of visual humour in Chapter 5 (Paint word pictures).

 ## REHEARSING A FEW 'AD-LIB' LINES

Rod Stewart sang about 'well rehearsed ad-lib lines'. You must be able to think on your feet, but it's always useful to know a few humorous lines you could use under the right circumstances.

During a wedding speech, you're most unlikely to be faced by loudmouth drunks or other nasty punters. And other interruptions, such as boisterous latecomers or early leavers, are likely to be minimal. However, these things can happen, and it is best to be prepared for them. So here are some mild lines that could prove useful to counter the kind of problems or distractions you could encounter:

- **Your microphone starts playing up**: 'Well, Mike, that's the end of our double act; I'm going solo.'
- **You fluff a line**: 'Sorry, I'm breaking these teeth in for the dog.'
- **You forget a name**: 'I'm so sorry, there are three things I always forget: names, faces and, er, . . . I can't remember the other.'
- **A glass smashes**: 'I'm pleased your having such a smashing time.'
- **To anyone leaving**: 'S/He'll be back in a wee while'.
- **To anyone returning**: 'Could you hear us out there? . . . we could hear you in here.'
- **A catch-all when anything goes wrong**: 'I hope that camcorder is still running. That's certain to be worth £250.'

But don't take the rise out of anyone until you've established yourself as the likeable, loveable chap that you are.

I would also counsel restraint; once you have responded to a friendly interruption or made a humorous remark about someone making a call of nature, it is best to get on with your speech and leave any further disruptions to go unnoticed.

MAKING WHAT MATTERS WORK FOR YOU

✓ Lighten your speech with touches of humour. Select a variety of relevant material that everyone present will find amusing.

✓ Take a few carefully targeted mild pot shots at the bridegroom . . . but make it patently clear to everyone that you don't really mean a word of it!

✓ Be more than just a talking head; wherever possible, act your jokes out.

✓ Be prepared to deliver one or two humorous 'ad-libs', should the circumstances demand them.

3 Being Congratulatory and Optimistic

Never overlook the five elements of a best man's speech which are almost impossible to overdo: welcome, congratulate, flatter, thank, praise.

3

things that
really matter

1 **SUGARING YOUR TEASING REMARKS WITH PRAISE**

2 **OFFERING ADVICE TO THE HAPPY COUPLE**

3 **WEAVING IN A COUPLE OF QUOTATIONS**

A speech that is all humour – however good the humour – can sometimes become tiresome and vacuous. You need some congratulatory and optimistic words to counterbalance your jokes and teasing remarks. Your speech needs to be underpinned by some good, old-fashioned sincerity. So **welcome** the guests, **congratulate** the newlyweds, **flatter** the bridesmaids, **thank** the hosts, and **praise** – well praise just about everyone and everything.

If it moves, praise it; if it doesn't move, praise it. Praise the hosts ('the nicest of people'), the groom ('the luckiest man in the world'), the bride ('doesn't she look radiant?'), the room ('these magnificent surroundings'), the occasion ('this wonderful event') and the meal ('it was nice to see the menu was in French – it made such a pleasant surprise each time the food arrived'). The good news is: there are ways of mixing and matching flattery with irreverent humour, so you don't need to be too nice for too long!

IS THIS YOU?

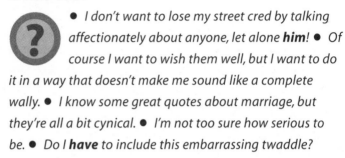

● *I don't want to lose my street cred by talking affectionately about anyone, let alone **him**!* ● *Of course I want to wish them well, but I want to do it in a way that doesn't make me sound like a complete wally.* ● *I know some great quotes about marriage, but they're all a bit cynical.* ● *I'm not too sure how serious to be.* ● *Do I **have** to include this embarrassing twaddle?*

① SUGARING YOUR TEASING REMARKS WITH PRAISE

The problem is that many of us are not very comfortable using gushing, extravagant language, especially when praising individuals. Fortunately, then, it's good to know that even effusive praise need not sound sycophantic in a speech.

The same flattery that could appear too florid or subservient when spoken in private seems quite acceptable in a public tribute. And your speech is a public tribute.

Funnily enough, a sincere compliment and a teasing jibe often fit well together, each reinforcing the other in a kind of verbal synergy. The trick is first to set up a situation which you can exploit with a teasing remark, before turning this into a genuine little compliment. If the praise comes immediately after the crowd has had a good laugh at the groom's expense, its effect on them will be at least doubled.

'When I asked (*groom*) about the wedding arrangements (*set-up*), he said, "Oh, I'll leave all that to you. But I do want Bells – and at least three cases of it (*tease*)." Well I don't know about Bells, but I work with (*groom*) at Grange Hill

Comprehensive – and I can tell you that he is certainly one of the best Teachers I know (*praise*).'

Alternatively, you may wish to build up the bridegroom with a public compliment before quickly bringing him down to earth with a bang. If so, you simply reverse your tease and praise.

'(*Groom*) is really quite well off (*set-up*). But he never brags about it (*praise*). In fact, you could sit in a pub with him all evening and never know he had a penny (*tease*).'

It's a comedy trick that works every time – set-up line, praise, teasing punchline. You draw the attention of the audience to your target – compliment them – and then comes that twist.

People are most affected by what they hear *last*. If you want to leave them with the compliment, then the formula is **set-up, tease, praise**. But if you want to leave them laughing, it's **set-up, praise, tease**.

 OFFERING ADVICE TO THE HAPPY COUPLE

As best man, you are expected to impart one or two pearls of wisdom to the newlyweds. Leave any really serious or emotional stuff to the bride's father, or to the groom, if they're that way inclined.

'There are two things that are vitally necessary if your marriage is to succeed. They are honesty and wisdom. Honesty: *always* – no matter what happens, no matter how adversely it may affect you – *always* keep your word to your partner once you have given it. Wisdom: *never* give your word.'

'Advice to the bridegroom? Easy. When she hands you a

dishcloth, blow your nose on it and hand it back.'

'Never go to bed angry . . . stay up and fight.'

'(*Groom*), if (*bride*) doesn't treat you as she should – be thankful.'

'Always remember the two little bears: bear and forbear. If you can bear up when times are hard – and forbear from losing your temper – there will be many anniversaries of this day to be celebrated in the years ahead.'

 WEAVING IN A COUPLE OF QUOTATIONS

Everyone enjoys hearing a particularly witty turn of phrase or apt quotation during a wedding speech. It can really lift a speech and it's a great way of saying the obligatory nice things about the groom without embarrassing yourself! You simply put your words and sentiments into someone else's mouth.

Try to avoid anything remotely negative, sneering or cynical. The problem is, many of the best quotes about love and marriage *are* negative, sneering or cynical. So if you feel you really *must* use one or two, reverse them to show this most definitely does *not* apply to the happy couple:

'Someone once said that he had gone into marriage with his eyes closed – her father had closed one of them and her brother had closed the other. Well, all I can say is that William went into his marriage with his eyes wide open. And seeing how Mary looks today, who could blame him?'

Very few quotes will be received with a knee-slapping bellylaugh. Their merit usually lies in their encapsulation of a truth, a smart observation or a humorous example.

Quotations are intended to promote smiles and nods rather than helpless mirth. For this reason, they should be spread thinly, like caviar, not piled on liberally, like marmalade. One or two quotes are plenty enough for any wedding speech.

Quoting people can sound pompous. Just give a couple of appropriate lines and do it in a very casual way. If you are quoting someone famous, it is a good idea either to make it clear you had to look it up, or to give the impression you're not absolutely sure of your source:

'I am reminded of the words of Groucho Marx – reminded, I should say, by Linda, who looked it up last night . . .'

'I think it was Bob Hope who said . . .'

If you want to quote someone less well known, don't mention him or her by name. If you do, the reaction will probably be an audible 'Who?' Rather, say something like:

'Someone once said . . .' or 'It has been said that . . .'

Alternatively, you could attribute the quotation to someone more famous. Oddly enough, this ploy will immediately increase your audience's appreciation of those words of wit and wisdom. But make sure the person you name sounds as if he *could* have said that. As Woody Allen didn't say, 'The key is to entertain, not to be factually accurate.'

Here are a few positive and optimistic quotations that you could weave into your speech:

Love and marriage
'Marriage is that relationship between man and woman in which the independence is equal, the dependence mutual, and the obligation reciprocal.' (*Louis K. Anspacher*)

'Partnership, not dependence, is the real romance in marriage.' (*Muriel Fox*)

'In the arithmetic of love, one plus one equals everything and two minus one equals nothing.' (*Mignon McLaughlin*)

The bride

'In most marriages, the woman is her husband's closest friend and adviser.' (*Helen Rowland*)

'Blest is the Bride on whom the sun doth shine.' (*Robert Herrick)*

'A woman is like a tea bag – you don't know her strength until she is in hot water.' (*Nancy Reagan*)

The groom

'Husbands are like fires – they go out when unattended.' (*Zsa Zsa Gabor*)

'The male is a domestic animal which, if treated with firmness and kindness, can be trained to do most things.' (*Jilly Cooper*)

'No self-made man ever did such a good job that some woman didn't want to make a few alterations.' (*Kim Hubbard*)

Second marriages

'Marriage is a lot like the army; everyone complains, but you'd be surprised at the large number that re-enlist.' (*James Garner*)

'Wedlock's like wine, not properly judged of till the second glass.' (*Douglas Jerrod*)

'The plural of spouse is spice.' (*Christopher Morley*)

And finally, a little more advice to the happy couple . . .

'Success in marriage is more than *finding* the right person; it is *being* the right person.' (*Rabbi B.R. Bricker*)

'To keep your marriage brimming
With love in the marriage cup,
Whenever you're wrong, admit it;
Whenever you're right, shut up.' (*Ogden Nash*)

'Laugh and the world laughs with you, snore and you sleep alone.' (*Anthony Burgess*)

MAKING WHAT MATTERS WORK FOR YOU

✓ Remember that it is almost impossible to be too optimistic or congratulatory. Use generosity, generously.

✓ Alternate friendly digs at the groom with genuine compliments.

✓ Offer a little light-hearted, humorous and optimistic advice to the newlyweds and include one or two relevant, positive, upbeat quotations in your speech.

4 Finding the Ideal Beginning and Ending

Think of your opening and closing words as the verbal bookends of your speech . . . they must be strong enough to hold and support everything that comes between them.

5

things that
really matter

1 **GRABBING THEIR ATTENTION**

2 **RESPONDING TO THE TOAST TO THE BRIDESMAIDS**

3 **ENDING ON THE RIGHT NOTE**

4 **READING THE TELE-MESSAGES**

5 **BRACKETING YOUR SPEECH**

There is no such thing as the *best* opening lines or the *best* closing lines for a best man's speech, because every speech – and every speaker – is different. In this chapter you will learn a number of techniques that can be used to open and close a speech. They are all tried and tested, so you don't need to worry about choosing a dud. Study the options and decide what would work best for *your* speech – and for *you*.

There are dozens of ways to put over a captivating opening, or to deliver a compelling close to a speech. It's just a matter of finding the pattern of words that suits your style and has exactly the effect you are after. Work on your lines until you've got them spot on. Then **memorise** them. You must know **precisely** how you are going to open and close your speech. There is absolutely no room for any ad-libbing here.

IS THIS YOU?

● The only opening and closing lines I can come up with are 'Good afternoon, Ladies and Gentlemen' and 'Thank you'. ● I'm not sure how I'm supposed to respond to the toast to the bridesmaids. ● I need to find an opening line that will make them laugh and make me relax. ● When I rehearse my speech, I find myself repeatedly announcing the end, which never seems to come. ● I want to top-and-tail my speech to make it sound really professional.

① GRABBING THEIR ATTENTION

It is vital to have an opening line that really grabs your audience's attention. Entertainers call this 'having a hook'. For the best man, undoubtedly, the most useful varieties of these are:

● the humour hook, and
● the anniversary hook.

Let's consider each of them:

The humour hook

A humorous opening is ideal for a best man's speech. But it must be fresh, to the point, told as succinctly as possible and timed so the punchline will elicit a laugh.

A self-depreciating opening always works – it puts the audience with you, not against you.

Here are some examples:

'Ladies and Gentlemen, I'm making this speech today under a considerable handicap – I'm sober.'

'Good Ladies, afternoon and Gentlemen . . . I *knew* I should have rehearsed this speech.'

'Ladies and Gentlemen, I won't take long. This suit has to be back in twenty minutes.'

'Ladies and Gentlemen, this is the first time I have spoken at a wedding reception – except during other people's speeches.'

'Ladies and Gentlemen, thank you, I appreciate your welcome because I just felt slightly unwell. I told (*groom*) that I was feeling funny and he said, "Well, do your speech before it wears off." '

'Ladies and Gentlemen, thank you. I'm not crazy about making speeches, but I've been going out with (*girlfriend*) for three years now and this is the first chance I've had to see if my voice still works.'

'Ladies and Gentlemen, (*groom*) told me that he wanted a best man capable of charming you with his spectacular wit, his staggering charisma and his dazzling personality. Well, I'm here to fill in while his search continues.'

'Ladies and Gentlemen, unaccustomed to public speaking as I am, I feel this irresistible urge to prove it.'

The anniversary hook

But if humour isn't your strong point, why not employ this classic opening gambit? There's nothing like telling people what a special day it is today. You're telling them that 'Today's the Day!' As always, use your own words, but this is the sort of thing you should say:

'Ladies and Gentlemen, this is an historic day! This day, the

13th of July, will always be remembered because of three world-famous events. Film actor Harrison Ford was born in 1942; Live Aid pop concerts raised millions for charity in 1985; and on this day in 200X, (*bridegroom*) married (*bride*)!'

'Ladies and Gentlemen, what a cosmic day! This very day, the 11th of August, will always be associated with three truly heavenly events. Two new moons were discovered around Mars back in 1877, our moon totally eclipsed the sun in 1999; and on this day in 200X, (*bride*) totally eclipsed everyone and everything. Doesn't she look radiant?'

'Ladies and Gentlemen, this is a truly historic day! This day, the 18th of June, will always be remembered because of three world-shattering events. Napoleon finally met his Waterloo, at Waterloo, in 1815; Sir Paul McCartney had his first day on earth in 1942; and on this day in 200X, you heard the finest best man's speech of your entire lifetime! Now – who's going to make it?'

You can find plenty of birthdays and anniversaries listed in specialist books (*Making a Wedding Speech*, in the How To Series, for example, has no less than 732 of them). You'll also find them in most daily and Sunday newspapers.

RESPONDING TO THE TOAST TO THE BRIDESMAIDS

Remember that tradition demands that you respond to the bridegroom's toast to the bridesmaids.

All that is required of you is a brief acknowledgement of the toast immediately before or soon after you hook your audience. Once that's out of the way you can forget it and get on with your speech.

'First of all, on behalf of the bridesmaids, I'd like to thank (*groom*), for his warm-hearted words. It really has been a pleasure for us all to have played a small part of your big day . . .'

'On behalf of all the attendants, I'd like to thank you sincerely for those generous words. Yes, the bridesmaids did a great job in helping (*bride*) up the aisle today . . . but she came to the church of her own free will.'

'Thank you, (*groom*), for those kind words about the bridesmaids and attendants, though I would have gone even further. They are the most delightful set of bridesmaids I have ever seen. Be honest, today you are blinkered and you only have eyes for (*bride*) – and who can blame you?'

Your opening sentence is the second most important sentence of your speech. Yes, you've guessed it: the most important sentence is your last.

 ENDING ON THE RIGHT NOTE

A wedding speech is like a love affair. Any fool can start it but to end it requires considerable skill. Your concluding remark should be to your speech what a high note is to an aria: the candescence that triggers applause. If you can find the ideal ending, you will inject that ultimate bit of magic.

Here are some classic closers that you could use, adopt or personalise. While you are not *expected* to propose yet another toast, it's a good idea to do so anyway.

'I must close now – I've got a fair bit to do back at the flat . . . (*bride and groom*), congratulations on finding each other. Many people search for years and decades for that one special person that will complete their joy. You're so fortunate to have found each other so early in life. Here's to complete happiness now and forever.'

'I must close now – I've got to get back to John O'Groats – and John's a very demanding lad . . . Ladies and Gentlemen, when two hearts are joined by true love, they both grow and mature into a miracle greater than either could be alone. Remember that always. A toast: two hearts are better than one.'

'Before I left home this morning, my little girl said to me: "Daddy, I hope they clap you and clap you and clap you after you speak. If they don't, I'll cry and cry and cry for ever and ever". Ladies and Gentlemen, I leave it to you – do you want to be responsible for a child being miserable for the rest of her life? . . . (bride and groom), may you have the hindsight to know where you've been . . . the foresight to know where you're going . . . and the insight to know when you've gone too far!'

'Marriage of two mature adults is really a meeting of two minds, of two hearts, of two souls . . . and of three cars, four pets, five rooms and six kids. It'll be a crowd of fun. Ladies and Gentlemen, let's drink a toast to all of them.'

'I leave you both with this thought: remember there are Seven Deadly Sins, enough for one each night . . . so have an enjoyable week's honeymoon! Ladies and Gentlemen, a toast . . .'

'As I said to the woman I lost my virginity to, thanks for laughing. Ladies and Gentlemen, please raise your glasses. Let's drink a toast to . . .'

'Before I sit down I'd like to thank you for being a wonderful audience . . . and you can feel proud because I'm very hard to please. Ladies and Gentlemen, a toast . . .'

 READING THE TELE-MESSAGES

If you are the last speaker, signal this by reading the tele-messages after finishing your speech (having first checked that they are not X-rated). Try to keep this final session interesting by giving some background details about the contents of the messages and about the people who sent them. Crack a joke or two, if the moment seems right.

As always, try to end on a particularly high note.

You could end with the funniest or most emotional message, or with one from some friends who live on the other side of the world, or perhaps with one from some very old family friends (in either or both senses of the phrase). Alternatively, you could simply **make up** the last message. However, if you do this, you must make it obvious to everyone that it *is* a joke:

'And finally, this one is from that old quill-pusher, William Shakespeare. And it says, "Sorry that I can't be with you today, but I'm Bard." Shakey goes on,' "It hath been said that all unhappy marriages are a result of the husband having brains. Verily, I have total confidence that this marriage will be an exceptionally happy one." '

You have reached your destination in style; it is now time to let them eat cake.

 BRACKETING YOUR SPEECH

This is a device usually associated with seasoned pros. It is designed not only to grab an audience's attention at the **start** of a speech, but also – and at the same time – to set up a situation that can be exploited at the **end**. The idea is to present your speech as a satisfying whole, not just as a series of jokes and stories, however well they may have been crafted and structured.

Bracketing is a wonderful way of linking an attention-grabbing opening with a humorous or romantic big finish.

The two brackets consist of a **set-up** at the opening of the speech and a **pay-off** at the end. The words you will end with include those planted clearly at the start, like this:

Set-up: Ladies and Gentlemen, when this little do ends, (*groom and bride*) are off to Texas. Where more appropriate for a cowboy builder to spend his honeymoon? He almost went to Texas once before, but they were closed so he went to B&Q instead.'

That's your first bracket. You've set up a situation briefly and then quickly reinforced it with two one-liners to make it more memorable. It's a pretty good humour hook in its own right, but there's more to come.

Pay-off: Well now that Texas honeymoon awaits them, so I suppose (*groom*) will be kissed in places he's only ever dreamt of before.'

Notice the repetition of the planted words 'Texas' and 'honeymoon'. This helps the open-and-closed nature of the brackets and provides a pleasing symmetry.

You could also use this technique to add a little compliment to sugar the teasing joke you opened with.

How about this sort of thing for the sporty types?

Set-up: Ladies and Gentlemen, as (*groom*) left the church today I heard him ask the vicar if he'd be committing a sin if he played tennis on the Sabbath. The vicar replied, "The way you play, it would be a sin on any day." But (*groom*) is improving. He practises by hitting a tennis ball against his garage door. It's really improved his game. He hasn't won yet, but last week he took the door to five sets.'

Pay-off: (*Groom and bride*) are excellent tennis players who are both game and set for the perfect match.'

You can get ideas for humorous or romantic brackets simply by listening to the best popular lyricists of yesterday and today: Sir Noel Coward, Ira Gershwin, Cole Porter, Sir Paul McCartney, Hal David, Marvin Hamlisch, Sir Tim Rice – to name but a few. This is how master songsmith Sammy Cahn achieved a nice little twist in the tale of 'Call Me Irresponsible':

Set-up: 'Call me irresponsible, call me unreliable, throw in undependable too.'

Pay-off: 'Call me irresponsible, yes I'm unreliable, but its undeniably true: I'm irresponsibly mad for you.'

However, if you make use of a composer's brackets, always **reword** them into the kind of language you use, making sure they **no longer rhyme**. In this way your audience won't recognise your source – or your sauce – and you are sure to come across as a natural and original speaker.

It is quite easy to adapt and paraphrase musical brackets to suit your speech. Let's take a more up-to-date example. These are the set-up and pay-off lines used by Rupert Holmes in 'Nearsighted':

Set-up: 'If you take these glasses from my face I think you will find I'm undeniably, certifiably just a shade blind. The day is brighter, somewhat lighter, when it's slightly blurred. Nearsighted, it's another lovely day, so I stumble on my way.'

Pay-off: 'Nearsighted: loving life is such a breeze. Nearsighted: I see just what I please – and it pleases me to see you. Though I'm slightly out of focus, I can see my dreams come true. Nearsighted? All I need to see is you.'

This is how a best man might adapt, develop and paraphrase these brackets when talking about a bespectacled bridegroom:

Set-up: 'Ladies and Gentlemen, they say love is blind. Well (groom) certainly can't see far ahead – not without his glasses – and I'm sure he'd be the first to admit that in the past at times he's been a bit shortsighted – and sometimes even made a bit of a spectacle out of himself – But today I'm sure, with or without his glasses, he can see his future mapped out very clearly.'

Pay-off: 'You know, today, for the first time in his life, (groom) doesn't need to wear his glasses to see what a bright and wonderful future lies ahead of him. And right now I'm sure he couldn't give a damn that he's a bit shortsighted. And why should he? – Love is blind. And anyway, all he needs to see is (*bride*) – But *we* need glasses – to drink a toast to the happy couple. Ladies and Gentlemen: to a bright future – to (*groom and bride*).'

MAKING WHAT MATTERS WORK FOR YOU

✓ Your opening is an opportunity. Grasp it. Devise a great opening that's spot on for **this speech, this audience** and **you**.

✓ Don't forget to respond early in your speech to the bridegroom's toast to the bridesmaids!

✓ End on just the right note. You need a big finish, a final round verbal k.o.

✓ Keep the guests interested and involved as you read the tele-messages.

✓ Consider bracketing your speech. Establish a memorable phrase at the beginning and then repeat it, with some amusing or thoughtful twist, at the end.

5 Putting it All Together

To create a great wedding speech requires excitement, empathy, warmth, enthusiasm – and flair. Flair is the sizzle in the sausage.

5

things that
really matter

1 **PREPARING YOUR SCRIPT**

2 **USING WORDS TO BE SAID, NOT READ**

3 **ADDING A SPARKLE TO YOUR SPEECH**

4 **REMEMBERING RHYTHM**

5 **KEEPING IT FLOWING**

Having something worthwhile to say is *never* enough. You need to know how to use words and images to reach your audience's minds and hearts. Your speech needs a touch of flair. Flair is partly intuition, which comes from experience, imagination and a willingness to think – and a careful study of this chapter!

If we face an important interview, we prepare ourselves to make the best possible impression. We *look* good. So, if we are about to meet an audience, we should polish our words as well as our shoes. We should *sound* good.

Today people's expectations are high and their attention spans are low. Merely to gain and hold an audience's attention requires flair. If you want to keep them interested, your speech must sparkle. So let's get polishing.

IS THIS YOU?

● *I don't know what sort of script to prepare – if any.* ● *The last time I made a wedding speech I think I must have sounded as if I was reading the news. I was too matter of fact.* ● *I want my speech to be more than just an unconnected series of jokes and reminiscences.* ● *Of course I want what I say to be entertaining, but I also want to use just the right words and expressions.* ● *I want to make my speech memorable – and for the right reasons!*

PREPARING YOUR SCRIPT

The best talkers are those who are most natural. They are easy, fluent, friendly and amusing. No script for them. How could there be? They are talking only to us and basing what they say on our reactions as they go along. For most of us, however, that sort of performance is an aspiration rather than a description. Our tongues are not so honeyed and our words are less winged. We need a script.

But what sort of script? Cards? Notes? Speech written out in full? It's up to you. There is no right way of doing it. Here is a simple method favoured by many speakers:

- Write the speech out **in full**.

- **Memorise** the opening and closing lines and **familiarise** yourself with the remainder of the speech.

- **Summarise** the speech on one card or one sheet of paper using **key words** to remind you of your **sequence** of jokes, anecdotes, quotations and so on.

The main advantage of this method is that the speaker will not only be sure to cover everything he wants to, but also come across as a natural and spontaneous speaker who is not merely reciting a prepared speech.

 ### USING WORDS TO BE SAID, NOT READ

Most people can write something to be *read*, few can write something to be *said*. Indeed, most people are unaware that there is even a difference.

We are used to writing things to be read: by our lecturers, our friends, our relatives, our bosses, our subordinates. Such everyday written communication is known as **text**. What we are *not* used to doing is speaking our written words out loud. Writing intended to be spoken and heard is known as **script**.

Every effective speaker *must* recognise that there are very important differences between text and script, namely:

Text	Script
• is a journey at the reader's pace	• is a journey at the speaker's pace
• can be re-read, if necessary	• is heard once, and only once
• can be read in any order.	• is heard in the order it is spoken.

Therefore, you must prepare a speech for an audience which *cannot* listen at its own pace; which *cannot* ask you to repeat parts it did not hear or understand and which *cannot* choose the order in which to consider your words.

The lesson is clear: **speak your words out loud before you commit them to paper**. You will find that each element, each phrase, each sentence, will be built from what has gone before. Instinctively, you will take your listeners from the **known** to the **unknown**; from the **general** to the **particular**; from the **present** to the **future**.

We seem subconsciously to understand the best words and phrases and the best order of words and phrases when we speak, but we seem to lose the knack when we write script.

Written words should be easy to **find**; **spoken** words should be easy to **remember**. Consider how the same sentiment might be conveyed, first using text and then script:

Text:
'The meaning of marriage is not to be found in church services, or in romantic novels or films. We have no right to expect a happy ending. The meaning of marriage is to be found in all the effort that is required to make a marriage succeed. You need to get to know your partner, and thereby to get to know yourself.'

Script:
'The meaning of marriage isn't to be found in wedding bells – it isn't the stuff of Mills and Boon romances – there is no happy every after. No, the meaning of marriage is in the *trying* and it's about learning about someone else – and through that, learning about yourself.'

③ ADDING A SPARKLE TO YOUR SPEECH

Use words and images creatively and originally and your speech will come to life. Things happen in the minds and hearts of your audience. If you look into their eyes, you can see it happen. It's a great experience.

- **Paint word pictures**. People today spend more time watching TV and films than listening to radio. They are used to **seeing pictures,** so you must give your speech a visual aspect, not just by telling a joke or story, but by painting word pictures that allow your audience's own imagination to take over. Don't merely tell a gag, paint it:

'A rather aged gent went into Tariq's Repairs. "I bought my TV in for repairs in 1990 but then the Old Bill paid me a visit and – well I only got out this morning," he explained, handing Tariq a very crumpled old ticket. Tariq retreated to the back room and was gone for about twenty minutes. He returned and handed the ticket back to the old man, saying, "We should have it ready for you by next week, sir." '

One mental picture is worth a thousand words.

- **Use figurative language**. Try to make your speech colourful and original. Similes and metaphors are particularly useful devices. A **simile** is a figure of speech, usually introduced by 'like' or 'as', that **compares** one thing to another:

'She was simmering *like* a corked volcano.'

Because a simile's function is comparison, it is not as evocative as a metaphor. A **metaphor** does not so much compare as **transform** one thing into another: The *right* metaphor can really lift a wedding speech:

'Marriage. Ever since humans gathered together in caves, they – we – have displayed a basic instinct for becoming couples. Your man and your woman. Your Romeo and Juliet. Your yin and your yang. It's as natural as his and hers bath towels. If the life of humankind were music it would all be duets. It's been a bit of a musical day one way and another. Violins in harmony with cellos, Debbie in harmony with Tony. The past in harmony with the future. And, as the Bard of Avon put it: "If music be the food of love, play on." '

- **Engage all the senses**. Sensory details bring breadth and depth to your descriptions. We can learn a lot from writers of popular fiction. This is how Stephen King brought a character to life in *Carrie*:

'Norma led them around the dance floor to their table. She exuded odours of Avon soap, Woolworth's perfume and Juicy Fruit gum.'

And how about this from Katherine Mansfield:

'Alexander and his friend in a train. Spring . . . wet lilac . . . spouting rain.'

So few words, yet the wetness is palpable.

As you speak, try to **involve** your audience. Allow them to do far more than just listen to you. Allow them to **experience** your speech.

 REMEMBERING RHYTHM

A good speech attracts and holds an audience as a magnet attracts and holds iron filings.

Here are another three techniques that will add an almost magical, melodic quality to your speeches:

- **The rule of three**. Three is a magic number. People love to hear speakers talk to the beat of three. The effect of three words, three phrases or three sentences is powerful and memorable:

'May you be blessed with happiness that grows . . . with love that deepens . . . and with peace that endures.'

'We wish you fun and excitement for today . . . hopes and dreams for tomorrow . . . and love and happiness forever.'

'May real joy fill your days . . . warm your nights . . . and overflow your hearts.'

- **Parallel sentences**. Sentences that are parallel add a rhythmic beauty that helps an audience anticipate and follow your thoughts:

'Marriage is a celebration of love. Marriage is a celebration of life. Marriage is a celebration of joy. As you walk through life, hold hands and never let go.'

- **Alliteration**. The repetition of sounds and syllables, usually at the beginning of words, can help create just the right mood. Your speech will become special and spellbinding:

'Water your garden with friendship and faith and favour. And then watch it grow. You deserve a garden of love.'

Using words colourfully and creatively will bring your speech to life like a shot of whisky in a cup of coffee.

 KEEPING IT FLOWING

Have you noticed how entertainers, politicians and TV presenters move **easily** and **unobtrusively** from one topic to another? Like them, you can make your speech flow **smoothly** and **gracefully** from beginning to end by making use of a few of these simple devices:

- **A bridge** is a word that alerts an audience that you are changing direction or moving to a new thought:

'So that's how Ed met Sophie. *But* romance didn't blossom right away . . .'

- **A trigger** is a repetition of the same word or phrase to link one topic with another:

'That was what Bill *was like* at school. Now I'll tell you what he *was like* at college . . .'

- **A rhetorical question** is a question which you ask – and answer:

'So that's the kind of man you've married, (*bride*). So what advice can I offer you to help keep him under control?'

Some members of the audience may know both the bride and bridegroom very well, while others may only know one of them. Asking a rhetorical question is also an excellent way of telling people something while not insulting the intelligence of those already in the know:

'What can I tell you about a man who won the school prize for economics, represented the county at hockey and passed his driving test – at the sixth attempt?'

- **A flashback** is a sudden shift to the past to break what seems to be a predictable narrative:

'We first met in . . .'

'We both worked for . . .'

'We became good friends when . . . (yawn, yawn!)

It would have been far more interesting to have provided an unexpected flashback link, such as :

'Today he's the confident, man-about-town you see before you. *But five years ago* he wasn't like that . . .'

- **A list** is a very simple way of combining apparently unrelated incidents:

'I remember three occasions when Tim got into trouble at school . . .'

But don't rely too heavily on lists because a catalogue of events soon becomes extremely tedious to listen to.

- **A pause** is a non-verbal way of showing your audience that you have finished one section of your speech and are about to move on to another.

- **A physical movement** is another non-verbal signal that you are moving on to something new. If you turn to the bride, your audience know that you are going to talk to her, or about her.

- **A quotation, joke or story** can also serve as an excellent link. Here a man-on-the bus gag links a personal compliment about good manners with a more general observation that everyone has played their part in making this a day to remember:

'(*Bride*) always shows good old-fashioned courtesy to her fellow human beings. A rare attribute today, I'm sure you'll agree. When she was on the bus last week she stood up to give an elderly gentlemen her seat. He was so surprised he fainted. When he came round he said "Thank you" and (*bride*) fainted. Well I'm delighted to say there has been absolutely no shortage of courtesy here today. Things could not have gone better . . . '

MAKING WHAT MATTERS WORK FOR YOU

✓ Rehearse using a variety of types of script – cards, notes, speech written out in full – before deciding which one suits you best.

✓ Think like a listener and write like a talker. Speak your words out loud before you commit them to paper.

✓ Use words and images creatively and imaginatively so they reach your audience's minds and touch their hearts.

✓ It is important that your words and expressions should be easy to listen to. Your speech should have its own rhythm.

✓ Make sure your speech flows **smoothly** and **gracefully** from beginning to end.

6 Delivering Your Speech

This above all: to thine own self be true.

3 things that really matter

1 **FINDING YOUR STYLE**

2 **GIVING OUT THE RIGHT NON–VERBAL MESSAGES**

3 **MAKING FEAR YOUR FRIEND**

What you say is so much more important than *how* you say it. A speaker without a powerful or melodious voice can register just as convincingly as a great orator as soon as the audience tunes into the fun and caring behind his words.

A little general advice on delivery technique can help smooth the edges without stifling individuality. But a great deal of so-called expert advice will remove the wonderfully imperfect distinctions about us and create unremarkable clones.

So while this chapter will stress the importance of projecting positive body language and having the right attitude to your speech, it will **not** put you in a strait-jacket of artificial presentation techniques. If you abandon everything that is natural to you and substitute 'acquired' mannerisms, you will come over as unnatural, awkward and insincere.

Essentially, you just need to be yourself – but **yourself made large**. If you offer your homage, your humour and your heart to listeners, they cannot resist.

IS THIS YOU?

● I've been told that my body language is very negative. ●The last time I made a speech it felt like I was standing aside from myself, listening to a voice that didn't belong to me. It was very strange. ● As I stand up in front of an audience a kind of lead veil comes over me and all I can see is a close-up of myself. I hear my voice in a very loud way and every word I utter sounds awful. ● When I speak in public, my voice dries up and it destroys all the natural flow, all the rhythms and any kind of creative spark or anecdote that might come in is destroyed. Terrible. ● I am extremely nervous about giving this speech.

FINDING YOUR STYLE

It is exceedingly difficult to discuss style and technique in general terms, since the ability to be entertaining and to tell jokes and stories is such a personal business. However, there are certain 'rules' and guidelines which appear to be universal. Here they are:

- **Make the speech 'yours'**. Did Elvis, Sinatra and Johnny Rotten all sound the same singing 'My Way'? Of course not. The artist makes the crucial difference. So, too, does the speaker.

The central dilemma facing many best men may be put thus: I want my speech to be funny, but I'm not a comedian. Unless you are a gifted comic, you can take the much simpler but equally effective course to win your laughs – play it straight. Leave broad comedy performance to the professional clowns. For most of us, the best way to tell a joke is to do so seriously.

But we all have *some* abilities and talents. Don't hide your light under a bushel. Any regional accents or dialects which you can do well (and only if you *can* do them well) should be incorporated into your stories. A punchline is doubled in effect in the appropriate Cockney or Brummie accent, especially after a 'straight' and serious build-up.

Have you any funny faces, impersonations or mannerisms of speech which infallibly convulse friends and relatives at parties? These eccentricities, suitably broadened out, might work just as well at the reception.

Whatever individual characteristics you have that are special to you should be nurtured and cultivated and worked on, for it is those personal and unique quirks of appearance, personality and expression that will mark you out as a speaker with something different to offer. And that is never a bad thing.

- **Be conversational.** When you are sitting leisurely, with family or friends, your conversation will be naturally relaxed and chatty, because that is the language of easy communication. When you make a best man's speech, the words you use should be more considered, imaginative, creative and rhythmical than your everyday language, yet the way you say them, the way you deliver your speech should remain unaffectedly relaxed and chatty.

If you 'put on an act', you will be perceived as phoney, boring or lacking in personality. As a result, you won't come over well. Certainly you may need to speak a little louder or make other concessions to accommodate the needs of your audience, but, in essence, nothing in your delivery style should change.

Casual conversation is not constructed in a literary way. You do not always finish your sentences. You repeat yourself. You use ungrammatical constructions – but you are obeying a different set of rules. You are obeying the rules of effective spoken communication which have been learnt, instinctively, down the ages. Don't abandon these rules when you speak in public.

The key, then, is to recognise what you are doing when you 'get it right' and achieve any successful communication, be it formal or informal, business or social, and then stay with it in any given situation, regardless of the stress level.

- **Be heard**. You must be **audible**. If you are not, all else is lost. If there is public address equipment available, find out how it works, get plenty of practice and then use it. If there is no sound-enhancing equipment, speak as clearly and as loudly as is necessary to be heard. If the only other person in the room was at the back, you would talk to him or her naturally, at the right level, without shouting or strain, by:

  - keeping your head up
  - opening your mouth wider than during normal speech
  - using clearer consonants
  - slowing down.

  If you remember that you must be heard by that same person, at the back, during your speech, however many other people may be in the room, you will make those same four **natural adjustments** to your delivery.

GIVING OUT THE RIGHT NON-VERBAL MESSAGES

We **speak** with our vocal cords, but we **communicate** with our whole body. An audience does a lot more than listen to a speech – it **experiences** it. Everything about a speaker's manner and demeanour contributes to the overall impression that the audience takes away.

Body language is potent. When you address a group of people they are constantly responding consciously and unconsciously to what your body is saying to them.

So what hidden messages do you give out when you speak? If you are unsure, watch yourself in a mirror, or ask a kind but critical friend. You will probably find that you need to work on one or more of the following:

- stance and posture
- movement and gestures
- eye contact and facial expression.

However, remember that while each of these may be considered in isolation, a positive change made to any of them will also have a direct and immediate positive effect on the others.

- **Stance and posture.** Your stance and posture are important. You are making a fundamental statement with your body. An aligned, upright posture conveys a message of confidence and integrity. Early man frightened his enemies by inflating his chest and spreading his arms to present a much wider profile (see Figure 1). Modern man uses exactly the same technique when he wants to convince others of his dominance (see Figure 2).

Fig. 1. The aggressive caveman.

This domineering stance is unsuitable for making a wedding. wedding speech.

A friendly, upright, open, unthreatening stance is far preferable.

Fig. 2. Don't threaten the guests!

Our instincts tell us that people who shield themselves – even with just their arms – are defensive (see Figure 3); while people who do not shield themselves are perceived as open and friendly (see Figure 4).

- **Movement and gestures**. You should be far more than just a talking head. You don't want to be so motionless that you look like a statue on loan from Madame Tussaud's. But, equally, you shouldn't attempt an impersonation of racing pundit John McCririck's arm-waving histrionics.

Fig. 3. The defensive cavewoman.

Crossed arms are
seen as defensive
and negative.

Open arms and open
palms are considered
friendly and positive.

Fig. 4. Don't defend yourself against the guests!

Try to identify any annoying movements or gestures which
you display. Do any of these faults apply to you?

- playing with your watch
- talking with your hand in front of your mouth
- pushing your glasses back up your nose
- jingling coins in your pocket
- waving your hands about for no reason
- rustling your notes
- shuffling your feet
- swaying
- making pointless gestures.

Try to eliminate any such habits because they are a powerful means of distraction. Your audience will become preoccupied with when they will happen next and will start **watching** you rather than **listening** to you.

Early man attacked his victims by holding a weapon above their heads and bringing it down with great force

Fig. 5. The hostile caveman.

(see Figure 5). Our legacy from this is that, even today, our ancestral memories perceive similar positions and movements as hostile (see Figure 6).

Here are a few sentences that could well be heard during a best man's speech. Speak them out loud and support your words with appropriate and expressive gestures. Watch yourself in a mirror, or ask friends how effective your gestures are:

'You know, I'm in a position to marry anyone I please. The problem is, I don't seem to be able to please anyone.'

'The time has come for me, too, to take a wife. The only question remains is: whose wife shall I take?'

'(*Groom*) told me he bought that suit for a ridiculous figure. Looking at him today, I'm afraid I must agree.'

Hands and fingers pointing upwards and finger-wagging sweeping movements are seen as threatening.

Open palms with fingers downward are seen as unthreatening and friendly.

Fig. 6. Don't be hostile to the guests!

'There's nothing I wouldn't do for (*groom*), and I know there's nothing he wouldn't do for me. In fact we spend our lives doing nothing for each other.'

'Ladies and Gentlemen, a toast: To love – the only game where a pair beats three of a kind.'

- **Eye contact and facial expression**. These are crucial aspects of effective communication because they gain and then maintain an audience's attention, create rapport, and give you valuable feedback as to how well you are coming over.

The worst you can do, apart from mumbling inaudibly, is not to look at your audience.

You should have **memorised** your opening and closing lines, so **look** at your audience as you deliver them. During the middle of your speech, try to keep your head up from your script for most of the time.

Entertainers use the so-called **lighthouse technique** to maintain eye contact with their audiences. This means beaming all around the room slowly, tracing an imaginary X or Z shape but continually varying the size and shape of the letter to avoid your eye sweeps becoming routine and predictable. Look at everyone and make this deliberate and noticeable. Stop occasionally to look at individuals for just long enough to give the impression that you are talking to them without picking them out for special attention.

But you must do more than simply look at your audience; you must use your eyes and your facial expression to convey your **feelings**. This isn't as difficult as it may sound. You do it every day. Practise using your eyes and facial expression to convey: happiness, optimism, mirth, joy, confidence, sincerity.

There is nothing more captivating than a smile. It shows warmth and friendliness and says, 'I'm really pleased to be making this speech. It's going to be great fun and we're all going to have a wonderful time!' So smile, smile – and smile again.

Once you begin to give out positive silent messages about your feelings and emotions, you will become even more enthusiastic and eager – and this, in turn, will be reflected in your body language. You will have broken into a wonderful virtuous circle.

*Positive body language not only **reflects** positive feelings, it **creates** them.*

 MAKING FEAR YOUR FRIEND

Fear is nothing to be frightened of. People get nervous because they are afraid of failing, of looking foolish, and not living up to expectations. Nervousness is caused by the fear of looking ridiculous to others.

Few speakers claim to be able to speak without any nerves. Some will say that lack of nerves is not only unlikely, it is undesirable. They need the adrenaline to carry them along. So how do you make things easier for yourself? First be assured that excessive worry is avoidable, if you follow this advice:

- **Rehearse**. Friends who tell you not to worry should worry you. Don't believe them when they say, 'No need to rehearse, it'll be alright on the night' – unless your hidden agenda is to get £250 from Lisa Riley for a camcorder calamity. If you want to calm your nerves and make a great speech, you simply *must* rehearse.

As with the type of script you use, so the rehearsal method you employ must be the one that best suits you. Some speakers like to be isolated and unheard in a distant room, with or without a mirror. Others perform their speeches again and again to a sympathetic spouse or friend, either encouraging suggestions from them, or requiring nothing more than a repeated hearing, to ease away inhibitions.

Rehearse your beginning and ending until you have got them spot on. Rehearse the body of your speech not to be perfect, but to be **comfortable**. Audiences don't expect you to be perfect, but they *need* you to be comfortable. If you're not comfortable, neither are they. And if they're not comfortable, they *cannot* be receptive to your words of wit and wisdom, however hard they may try.

Why do some actors freeze or fumble on the opening night and then pick up a British Theatre Drama Award six months later? It's a fear of unfamiliarity. As the days, weeks and months go by, the fear abates and the quality of the performance improves.

The more rehearsal, the more the certainty of success and greater peace of mind.

Words become more familiar. Awkward juxtapositions are smoothed out. You suddenly think of a way of saying a stuffy sentence in a more straightforward and colloquial style. At the same time you will recognise the parts of your speech that hit the spot, the parts that require a little fine tuning, and the parts that are simply not worth including.

- **Have the right attitude.** Tell yourself that you are going to make a great little speech. And *believe* it. The largely untapped power of positive thinking really is enormous. It has been estimated that 85 per cent of performance is directly related to **attitude**. Unfortunately, many speakers think they are going to fail and, with this attitude, this becomes a self-fulfiling prophesy.

Approach your speech with confidence, courage and conviction.

- **Visualise success.** Visualisation is the planting of mental images into the subconscious mind. These images must be vivid and real – you must be able to **see**, to **hear**, to **smell**, to **touch**, to **taste** and to truly **live them**.

*If you can vividly **imagine** an event happening, it will greatly strengthen the likelihood of it **actually** happening.*

This is not a crankish idea. Controlled medical experiments have proved it to be true. When a patient visualises cancer cells being engulfed by anti-bodies in the bloodstream, it is far more likely to happen than if that patient just lies back and lets nature take its course.

So reinforce your positive attitude with a positive visualisation of your speech. Imagine yourself talking in a relaxed and confident manner. You are looking good. They love your opening hook. But it gets better: your stories and jokes wow them. They are eating out of your hand. Then comes that big finish. Nobody could have topped that. Listen to their cheers and applause. Now that's what I call a wedding speech!

- **Be prepared for the worst**. Even the best-prepared and most psyched-up speaker can suffer from a sudden attack of the collywobbles on the big day. You must be prepared for this possibility. This does *not* reflect a negative attitude, it reflects a sensible one.

Taking out an insurance policy does not mean you expect to fall down a manhole or to be struck by lightning.

If you feel the pressure getting to you remind yourself that this is a happy occasion. The audience is on your side. They are willing you to do well. If you are *still* feeling over-anxious, try this simple emergency relaxation technique:

- Pull in your stomach muscles tightly. Relax.
- Clench your fists tightly. Relax.
- Extend your fingers. Relax.
- Press your elbows tightly into the side of your body. Relax.
- Push your feet into the floor. Relax.

However, always remember that the greatest antidotes to nerves are preparation and attitude. If you prepare well and have a positive attitude, what you used to call fear can be renamed excitement and anticipation.

MAKING WHAT MATTERS WORK FOR YOU

✓   The challenge is to project your personality, not suppress it. Knowing that you not only *can*, but also *should* 'be yourself' will stop you worrying about your 'performance', and allow you to concentrate on what really matters: being yourself and entertaining your audience.

✓   The effectiveness of your speech will depend, to a large extent, on your body language. A relaxed stance and upright posture, purposeful economy of movement, fluid gestures and lively eyes and facial expression will all capture your audience's attention and greatly enhance the impact of your speech.

✓   Whether you think you will succeed or whether you think you will fail, you will probably be right!

7 Stories, Jokes and One-liners For Your Speech

A newspaper hack once asked, 'Why let the facts get in the way of a good story?' Good question. And, when it comes to wedding speeches at least, the answer is that they shouldn't. Well, to a point! Remember that a story must sound as if it *could* be true. This is particularly important if you refer to people in the room – and you *should* try to bring in a few of the personalities who are at the reception, especially those seated at the top table.

The audience must think to itself, 'Yes, the bridegroom may well have said that,' or 'the bride could well have done that under those circumstances.' In other words, a story must have a ring of truth about it. There is no point in telling the most hilarious joke about the groom's incredible drinking exploits if everyone in the room knows his idea of a heavy night out on the town is two halves of lager and a packet of cheese and onion crisps.

This chapter provides a miscellany of jokes and humorous stories which can be told as they appear, or can be adapted and personalised to suit the occasion. I will provide you with plenty of material ranging from mild one-liners to quite saucy stories which sensitive souls may find rather raw. Only you know how broadminded the crowd is likely to be, so choose your stories and jokes with care. Use your own judgement and common sense and perhaps take advice from the bride and groom.

Many of the best stories and jokes about love and marriage are quite cynical, and there is absolutely no place for anything negative or sneering in a wedding speech. A simple way to get around this dilemma is to make it abundantly clear that any cynical views expressed in your jokes most certainly do *not* apply to the happy couple, like this:

'Someone once said that a successful marriage depends on the husband falling in love several times. I'm sure Nick agrees, only he would add four more words. A successful marriage depends upon a husband falling in love several times . . . with the same women!'

Finally, always apply the Bob Monkhouse Test to potential material (see page 17).

1. Do *you* think it is funny?
2. Can you say it confidently and with comfort?
3. Is there any danger of offending anyone?
4. Will they understand and appreciate it?

If a story joke, or one-liner passes this test with flying colours, it could well merit a place within your speech. Now for the jokes:

The trouble with being the best man at a wedding is that you never get the chance to prove it.

Some newly married friends were visiting us and the topic of children came up. The bride said she wanted three children while the husband said two would be enough for him. They discussed this discrepancy for a few minutes until the husband thought he would put an end to things by saying boldly, 'After our second child I'll just have a vasectomy.' Without a moment's hesitation the bride retorted, 'Well I hope you'll love the third child as if it were your own.'

Ian plays for Melchester Rovers in the Sunday League. They've tried him in every position, but he's useless at all of them. Jayne, we wish you better luck.

A boy is about to go on his first date and is nervous about what to talk about. He asks his father for advice. The father replies, 'My son, there are three subjects that always work: food, family and philosophy.' The boy picks up his date and they go to a burger bar. They stare at each other for a long time over a pair of Big Macs as the boy's nervousness builds. He remembers his father's advice and chooses the first topic: Food. He asks the girl, 'Do you like spinach?' She says 'no' and the silence returns. After a few more uncomfortable moments, the boy thinks of his father's suggestion and turns to the second item on the list: Family. He asks, 'Do you have a brother?' Again, the girl says 'no' and there is more awkward silence. The boy then plays his last card. He thinks of his father's advice and turns the conversation to Philosophy. He asks the girl, 'If you had a brother, would you like spinach?'

I've been told that 80% of married men cheat in Britain. The rest take the Eurotunnel and cheat in France.

Jack and Vera are celebrating their 50th wedding anniversary. Jack says to Vera, 'Tell me, dearest, have you ever cheated on me?' 'What a question!' Vera replies. 'Do you really want to know?' 'Yes', responds Jack. 'Very well,' she says, 'then I shall tell you. I have cheated on you three times.' 'Three? Well, when were they?' he replies. 'Remember when you were 35 and the bank refused you a loan to start your own business?' she begins, 'and then the bank manager came to our house and signed the papers, no questions asked?' 'Oh, Vera, you did that for me. I respect you more than ever to do such a thing. When was the second time?' he asks. 'Remember when you were 40 and you needed a triple heart bypass operation, but the waiting list was too long to wait and we couldn't afford to go private?' she asks, 'and then Dr Morgan travelled here from London and performed the operation personally the next week?' 'I can't believe it, Vera,' he says, 'you did that to save my life? What a wonderful wife you are! Tell me about the third time.' 'Well, Jack,' she continues, 'remember when you were 45, and you really wanted to be President of the golf club but you were 19 votes short. . .?'

Gavin doesn't know the meaning of the word meanness. Mind you, he doesn't know the meaning of lots of other words either.

A man gets married and shortly afterwards his wife dies. A friend tries to console him and asks, 'What happened to your wife?' 'She died of poison from eating mushrooms,' says the husband. The man gets married a second time, and not long after the marriage, this second wife dies. The same friend tries to console the grieving husband and asks, 'What happened to your second wife?' 'She died of poison from eating mushrooms,' comes the reply from the husband. The man takes a third wife and, not very long after the marriage, the third wife dies. The consoling friend asks, 'What happened to your third wife? Was it mushroom poisoning?' The grieving husband responds, 'No, she died of a broken neck.' 'A broken neck!' replies the friend. 'Yes,' says the husband, 'she wouldn't eat the mushrooms.'

There is no doubt about it, men have better taste than women. After all, Paul chose Christina – but Christina chose Paul.

A young couple were called to Heaven before they could be married. The disappointed groom took St Peter aside and asked him if it was possible for them to be married. 'I'm afraid you'll have to wait,' St Peter replied, 'Ask me again in five years time, and if you still want to be married, we'll talk about it then.' Five years passed and the couple came back to see St Peter, repeating their request. St Peter replied, 'Sorry, but you must wait another five year.' Fortunately, after the wait, St Peter said they could be married. The wedding was beautiful and at first the couple were very happy, but later they realised they had made a mistake. They went to see St Peter, this time to ask for a divorce. 'What?' St Peter asked, 'It took us ten years to find a *Minister* in Heaven. What chance is there of finding a *lawyer*?'

You may have noticed how few single people were invited to the wedding. I'll let you into a secret: that was Ray's idea. He's very astute. He told me that if he invited only married people, all the presents would be clear profit.

A Chinese couple get married. On the wedding night the groom says, 'I will do whatever pleases you. Tell me, what do you want?' Without hesitation, she replies, 'I want 69.' He looks at her for a moment and then asks, 'With noodles or bean sprouts?'

A newlywed farmer and his wife were visited by her mother who immediately demanded an inspection of the place. The farmer had genuinely tried to get on with his new mother-in-law, hoping that it could be a friendly, non-antagonistic relationship. But all to no avail though, as she kept nagging them at every opportunity, demanding changes, offering advice and generally making life unbearable for the farmer and his new bride. While they were walking through the barn during the enforced inspection, the farmer's horse suddenly reared up and kicked the mother-in-law in the head, killing her instantly. It was a shock to them all, no matter what their feelings towards her, and her demanding ways. At the funeral service a few days later, the farmer stood near the coffin and greeted people as they entered the church. The vicar noticed that whenever a woman would whisper something to the farmer, he would nod his head and say something; whenever a man walked by and whispered to the farmer, however, he would shake his head and mumble a reply. Very curious as to this bizarre behaviour, the vicar later asked the farmer why he responded so differently to men and women. The farmer replied, 'The women would say, "What a terrible tragedy," and I would nod my head and say "Yes it was." The men would ask, "Can I borrow your horse?" and I would shake my head and say, "Sorry, you can't, it's already been booked up for the whole year.' "

There's absolutely nothing wrong with Steve that a miracle can't cure.

A man and his wife enter the dentist's surgery. 'I want a tooth pulled,' the man says, 'and we're in a big hurry so let's not waste time with injections or gas or anything like that, let's just pull it out.' 'You're a very brave man,' remarks the dentist,' which tooth is it?' 'Show him your bad tooth, darling', says the man to his wife.

The girl asked her lover, 'Darling, if we get engaged, will you give me a ring?' 'Of course,' replied the lover, 'what's your phone number?'

A man is sitting at the bar, drinking a double Scotch, when an attractive woman sits down beside him. The barman serves her an orange juice and the man turns to her and says, 'This is a special day. I'm celebrating.' 'I'm celebrating too,' she replies, clinking glasses with him. 'What are you celebrating?' he asks. 'I've been trying to have a child for years,' she answers, 'and today my gynaecologist told me I'm pregnant.' 'Congratulations,' the man says, lifting his glass, 'as it happens I'm a chicken farmer and for years all my hens have been barren, but today they're finally fertile.' 'How did it happen?' she asks. 'I changed cocks,' comes the reply. 'What a coincidence,' she says, smiling.

The stewardess told the passenger, 'I'm sorry, sir, but we left your wife behind in Paris.' 'Thank goodness,' replied the man, 'I thought I'd gone deaf!'

A man was telling his friend that he and his wife had had a furious row the night before. 'But it ended,' he said, 'when she came crawling to me on her hands and knees,' 'What did she say?' asked the friend. The husband replied, 'She said, "Come out from under the bed, you coward!"'

Dave made that speech for nothing ... and I'm sure you'll agree, it was worth every penny.

A mother has three daughters. As each of them gets married, she asks them to write, as soon as possible, about how married life is treating them. To avoid embarrassment to their new husbands by openly discussing their love lives, the mother and daughters agree to use newspaper advertisements as a code to let the mother know how things are going. The first girl gets married and the letter duly arrives within a few days with the simple message: 'Maxwell House Coffee'. The mother gets the newspaper and checks the Maxwell House advertisment which says: 'Satisfaction to the last drop'. So the mother is happy. The second daughter gets married. After a week there is a message which says: 'Slumberland Matresses'. So the mother checks out the ad which says: 'Full Size, King Size'. So the mother is happy. Then it comes to the time of the third daughter's wedding. The mother hears nothing and is anxious. After two months comes the message: 'British Airways'. The mother looks up the ad, but this time she faints. The ad reads: 'Three times a day, seven days a week, both ways'.

A woman was telling her friend, 'It was I who made my husband a millionaire.' 'And what was he before you married him?' asked the friend. The woman replied 'A billionaire.'

A woman was getting married for the fourth time, but claimed still to be a virgin. During her hen night, her girlfriends asked her how this could be. The woman replied, 'It's true. I am a virgin. My first husband was a psychologist. He just wanted to talk about it. My second husband was a gynaecologist. He just wanted to look. My third husband was a stamp collector. God, I miss him!'

It only takes one drink to get Steve drunk – the fourteenth.

A man and woman who have never met before find themselves in the same sleeping compartment on the overnight train to Edinburgh. After their initial embarrassment, they both manage to get to sleep, the woman on the top bunk, the man on the lower. In the middle of the night the woman leans over and says, 'I'm sorry to bother you, but I'm awfully cold and I was wondering if you could possibly pass me another blanket.' The man leans out and with a glint in his eye, and says, 'I've got a better idea ... let's pretend we're married.' 'Why not?' giggles the woman. 'Good,' he replies, 'get your own blanket.'

Jim is very responsible. If there is a problem, you can be sure he's responsible.

Dave got out of the lift on the 20th floor and nervously knocked on his blind date's door. She opened it and was as beautiful and charming as everyone had said. 'I'll be ready in a few minutes,' she said, 'why don't you play with Fido, my dog, while you're waiting. He does wonderful tricks: he rolls over, shakes hands, and if you make a hoop with your arms, he'll jump through.' The dog followed Dave onto the balcony and started rolling over. Dave made a hoop with his arms and Fido jumped through, but right over the balcony railing. Just then Dave's date walked out. 'Isn't Fido the nicest, happiest dog you have ever seen?' she asked. 'To tell the truth,' Dave replied, 'Fido seemed a little depressed to me.'

Old Farmer Jones was dying. The family were standing

around his bed. With a low voice, he said to his wife, 'When I'm dead I want you to marry Farmer Brown.' 'No, I can't marry anyone after you,' she replied. 'But I want you to,' he said. 'Why?' she asked. 'Because he cheated me once on a horse deal,' came the reply.

At a cocktail party, one woman said to another, 'Aren't you wearing your wedding ring on the wrong finger?' The other replied, 'Yes,' I am. I married the wrong man.'

A man asked his married friend whether he had ever suspected his wife of leading a double life. 'I certainly do,' the married man replied, 'hers and mine.'

At the Gates to Heaven a new arrival noted that there were two paths, one marked Women, and one marked Men. He took the latter path and found that led to two gates. The gate on the left had a sign that said: Men Who Were Dominated By Their Wives. The gate on the right had a sign which said: Men Who Dominated Their Wives. The left-hand gate had a long line of men waiting, but there was only one scrawny little chap at the right-hand gate. The new arrival, before deciding which gate to go to, went over to the scrawny man and asked, 'Are you standing here because you were the dominant partner in your marriage?' 'Not really,' came the reply, 'I'm standing here because my wife told me to.'

Pete's a man of rare gifts. He hasn't given one in years.

A man and woman were married for forty years. When they were first wed, the man said, 'I am putting a box under the bed and you must promise not to look into it!' In all of their forty years of marriage the woman never looked. However, on the morning of their fortieth wedding anniversary curiosity got the better of her and she lifted the lid and peeked inside. In the box were three five pound notes and a building society passbook with a balance of £2400. She closed the box and put it back under the bed. Now that she knew what was in the box, she was doubly curious as to why. That evening they went out to a special dinner at their favourite restaurant. After their meal the woman could no longer contain her curiosity and confessed, saying, 'I'm so sorry. For all these years I've kept my promise and never looked. However, today, the temptation was too much and I gave in. But now I need to know why you keep cash in that box.' The man thought for a while and said, 'I suppose that after all these wonderful years you deserve to know the truth. Whenever I was unfaithful to you I put a five pound note in the box under the bed to remind me not to do it again.' The woman was shocked and said, 'I am very disappointed and saddened, but I suppose that after all those years away from home, on the road, temptation does happen and three times isn't so bad given all the years involved.' They hugged and made their peace. A little while later the woman asked the man, ' Why do you keep so much money in that Abbey National account?' To which the man answered, 'Whenever the notes built up to £200, I put it into the building society.'

I'm supposed to sing the bridegroom's praise and tell you all about his good points. Unfortunately, I can't sing, and I can't think of any good points.

A couple decided that the only way to have a Sunday afternoon quickie with their 10-year-old son in the flat was to send him out on the balcony and order him to report on all the neighbourhood activities. The boy began his commentary as his parents put their plan into operation. 'There's a few kids playing football in the park,' he said, 'and an ice cream van just drove by.' A few minutes passed. 'Looks like the Browns are having visitors,' he called out. 'Lucy's riding her new bike and the Smiths are having sex.' From the bedroom his startled father enquired, 'How do you know that?' 'Their kid is standing on the balcony too,' replied the son.

A man gets home, runs into the house, slams the door and exclaims, 'Pack your bags, I've won the lottery!' The wife says, 'Incredible! Should I pack for the country or for the coast?' He says, 'I don't care, just pack and get out!'

A man is dating three women and he can't decide which one to marry. He gives each £500 to see how well they can handle money. The first one spends £400 and puts £100 in the bank. The second one spends £100 and puts £400 in the bank. The third one puts all £500 in the bank. Which one does he end up marrying? The one with the biggest boobs.

Debs finds Doug very attractive. Then again, she is on heavy medication.

A deaf couple are on their honeymoon. The husband asks his wife, in sign-language: Honey, how would I tell you when I want to have sex? The wife replies in sign: If you want to have sex, bite my right nipple once; if you don't want to have sex, bite my left nipple twice. Accepting this method, the wife asks the same question to her husband. The husband replies: Darling, if you want to have sex, pull my willy once; if you don't want to have sex, pull my willy twenty seven times.

A jockey and his new bride ask the hotel receptionist for a room. 'Congratulations on your wedding,' the receptionist says, 'would you like the bridal then?' 'No thanks,' says the jockey, 'I'll just hold her by the ears till she gets the hang of it.'

A man receives a message that his mother-in-law has died and he is asked whether she should be buried or cremated. He says, 'Don't take any chances. Burn the body and bury the ashes.'

Every once in a while we have the opportunity to talk of a man of high achievement, transparent integrity and penetrating intellect. Not today though.

A man's wife asks him to go to the shop to buy some cigarettes. He walks down to the shop only to find it's gone 8 o'clock and the shop's closed. So he goes into a nearby pub to use the vending machine. At the bar he sees a beautiful woman and starts talking to her. They have a couple of drinks, one thing leads to another and they end up back at her place. After they have had their fun, he realises that it's almost midnight and he thinks: 'Oh no, my wife is going to kill me!' So he takes a piece of snooker cue chalk from his pocket and rubs it over his hands and then goes home. His wife is waiting for him in the doorway.

'Where the hell have you been?' she exclaims. 'Well, darling,' he says, 'it's like this. I went to the shop like you asked, but it was gone eight so they were closed. So I went to the pub to use the vending machine. I saw this great looking girl there. We had a few drinks, one thing led to another and I ended up in bed with her.' 'I don't think so,' says the wife, 'let me see your hands.' She sees his hands are covered with blue chalk and says, 'You liar, you've been playing snooker down the club again!'

Ronnie is so unlucky, even if he were to be reincarnated he'd probably come back as himself.

A couple were getting ready to go to bed and when the husband came in from the bathroom his wife was rubbing cream all over her boobs. He asked, 'What are you doing?' and she replied, 'I'm not happy with the size of my breasts and this cream is supposed to make them larger. But I don't think it's working.' He said, 'Wait a minute, I have an idea.' He went back into the bathroom and came out with a few sheets of toilet paper and started rubbing them over her boobs. She asked, 'What are you doing?' He replied, 'Well you have been wiping your bum with this stuff for years and look how big that has got.'

I have to tell you that in all the years I've known him, no one has ever questioned John's intelligence. In fact, I've never heard anyone mention it.

There was this couple who spent more than they earned and were always getting into financial difficulties. One day they came up with an idea. Each time they have sex they will put a £10 note in a piggy bank and this will eventually pay for the holiday they dream of. They buy the piggy bank and follow the agreed plan. After a time they think they must have enough cash saved to be able to book their Carribean cruise, so they break open the piggy bank. The husband looks at their savings and says, 'Isn't it strange, each time we have sex, I put a £l0 note into the piggy bank, but we also have many £20 notes and a few £50's.' The wife replies, 'Do you think all men are as stingy as you?'

Noel is a man of hidden talents. I just hope some day he'll find them.

A man is reading his newspaper when his wife walks up behind him and smacks him on the back of his head with a frying pan. He asks, 'What was that for?' She says, 'I found a piece of paper in your pocket with "Billie Jo" written on it.' He says, 'Don't be silly, love, that was the name of the horse I went to the bookies to back last week.' She shrugs and walks away. Three days later he is reading his newspaper when she walks up behind him and again smacks him on the back of the head with the frying pan. He asks, 'What was that for?' She answers, 'Your horse just phoned you.'

What's the difference between a boyfriend and a husband? About three stone.

'I must take every precaution not to get pregnant,' said Tracy to Sharon. 'But I thought you said your hubby had a vasectomy,' Sharon responded. 'He did. That's why I have to take every precaution.'

A recent survey done by marriage experts shows that the most common form of marriage proposal these days consist of the words: 'You're what?!'

A newlywed wife tells her husband, 'Darling, that young couple that just moved in next door seem so loving. Every morning, when he leaves the house, he kisses her goodbye and every evening, when he comes home, he brings her a dozen roses. Now why can't you do that?' 'Gosh,' her husband replies, 'I hardly know her.'

Bill and his new friend Ben were having a drink together and were talking about their respective married lives. 'I had sex with my wife before we were married,' said Bill, 'did you?' 'I don't know,' replied Ben, 'What was your wife's maiden name?'

A Russian, an Italian and an Irishman decide to go for a drink. Boris says, 'Let's go to Gorkys. With every third round the barman will give us a free vodka.' Giuseppe says, 'That sounds good, but if we go to Pavarottis with every third round they bring us a free bottle of wine to the table.' Paddy says, 'That sounds fine, but if we go to O'Learys we drink for free all night and then we go into the car park and get laid.' 'That sounds too good to be true,' Boris exclaims, 'Have you actually been there?' 'No,' Paddy replies, 'but my wife goes there all the time.'

Louise, pregnant with her first child, paid a visit to her obstetrician. After the examination, she shyly began, 'My husband wants me to ask you...' 'I know. I know,' the doctor said, placing a reassuring hand upon her shoulder, 'I get asked that all the time. Sex is fine till late in pregnancy.' 'No, that's not it,' Louise confessed, 'he wants to know if I can still mow the lawn.'

If I ever need a brain transplant, I'd choose Jim's . . . because I'd want one that had hardly been used.

A woman is talking on the phone: 'That's fine, sweetheart. No problem. I hope you have a good time. See you later.' Then she puts down the receiver. 'Who was that?' asks the man laying beside her in bed. 'My husband,' she replies. 'What did he want?' he enquires. 'Nothing,' she answers, 'he said he would be home later today. He's down the pub playing darts with you and some other friends.'

'Will I be the first to do this to you?' he whispers to his bride on their wedding night. 'Silly boy,' she replies, 'how could I know, you have not told me which position you are going to use.'

Tim sent his photograph off to a Lonely Hearts Club. They sent it back, saying they weren't that lonely.

They were married, but since the argument they had a few days earlier, they hadn't been talking to each other. Instead they were giving each other written notes. One evening he gave her a piece of paper which said: 'Wake me up tomorrow morning at 6 am'. The next morning he woke up only to find that the time was 9 o'clock. Naturally, he got very angry. As he turned around he found a note on his pillow saying: 'Wake up it's 6 o'clock'.

My ambition is to be the last man on earth – so that I can find out if all those girls were telling the truth.

As he lay on his deathbed, a man confided to his wife, 'I cannot die without telling you the truth: I cheated on you throughout our entire marriage. All those nights when I told you I was working late I was with other women, and not with just one woman either, I have slept with dozens of them.' His wife looked at him calmly and said, 'Why do you think I gave you the poison?'

During a heated argument over finances, the Duke said, 'Well, if you learned to cook and were willing to clean this place, we could fire the maid.' The Duchess, fuming, shot back, 'That may be true, but if you learned how to make love, we could fire the chauffeur and the gardener.'

The newlywed wife said to her husband when he returned home from work, 'I have great news for you. Pretty soon there will be three of us in this house, not two.' Her husband ran to her with a huge smile on his face and delight in his eyes. He was glowing with happiness and kissing his wife when she said, ' I'm glad you feel this way, because my mother's moving in tomorrow.'

A young couple were on their honeymoon. The husband was sitting in the bathroom, on the edge of the bath, saying to himself: 'How can I tell my wife that I've got really smelly feet and that my socks absolutely stink? I've managed to keep it from her while we were dating, but now she's bound to find out. How can I tell her?' Meanwhile his wife was sitting on the bed, saying to herself: 'How can I tell my husband that I've got really bad breath? I managed to keep it from him while we were courting, but now he's bound to find out. How can I tell him?' The husband finally plucks up the courage to tell his wife. He walks across the bedroom, puts his arms around her neck, moves very close to her face and says, 'Darling, I have a confession to make . . .''So have I, love,' she interrupts. To which he replies, 'Don't tell me you've eaten my socks!'

A man had dated a woman about once or twice a week for over twenty years. He really loved her, but he was just too timid to propose. One day he finally decided that life was too short. He would take the plunge and pop the question. What had he to lose? So he called her on the phone. 'Mary?' 'Yes, this is Mary.' 'Mary, will you marry me?' he asked. 'Of course I will,' she replied, 'Who am I speaking to?'

The blind date goes extremely well and at the end of the evening, as they begin to undress each other in his flat, the man says, 'Before we go any further, Sue, do you have any special fetishes that I should take into account in bed?' 'As a matter of fact,' smiles the girl, 'I do have a foot fetish, but I suppose I'd settle for seven or eight inches.'

During that heatwave a few years ago, as he stepped out of the shower, Robin said, 'It's just too hot to wear clothes. What do you think the neighbours would say if I mowed the lawn like this?' His wife replied, 'Probably that I married you for your money.'

A young married couple drove ten miles down a country road, not saying a word. An earlier discussion had led to an argument and neither wanted to concede their position. As they passed a farmyard of pigs and mules, the husband sarcastically asked, 'Are they relatives of yours?' 'Yes,' his wife replied, 'I married into the family.'

A little girl at a wedding asks, ' Mummy, why do brides wear white?' Her mum replies, 'Because they're happy, dear.' Halfway through the wedding the girl whispers, 'Mummy, if brides wear white because they're happy, then why do men wear black?'

As you all know, Mark is a successful salesman and last year he won the Salesperson of the Year award. When Mark's company presented him with the award, they arranged to have a guest speaker that would be in keeping with the Company's image of being great pioneers in their field. This was the famous Neil Armstrong. As an extra reward to Mark, he got to meet Armstrong. The great astronaut told Mark this story. When Apollo 11 landed on the moon, back in 1969, NASA televised the images to the world and Armstrong spoke those immortal words: 'That's one small step for man. One giant leap for mankind.' But what he told Mark was that NASA had actually edited out some of what he'd said and that what nobody else in the world had heard was that he went on to say: 'And good luck to Mr Martelli.' Of course, Mark asked what he meant by: 'And good luck to Mr Martelli.' Armstrong explained that when he was a little boy, growing up in Ohio, he lived with his parents in a modest terraced house. Armstrong said that he always remembered, as he lay in bed one night, hearing his next door neighbour Mrs Martelli saying to her husband, 'Go to sleep, Giuseppe, you've got as much chance of a blow job as the little boy next door walking on the moon!'

8 Sample Speeches

Finally, it's time to put it all together by taking a look at some full length speeches. While you may decide to adapt, personalise, and possibly combine what you consider to be the best bits, the main reason for including them in this final chapter is to remind you of the style and tone you should adopt throughout your speech. Your address should be upbeat, congratulatory, humorous ... and *short*. Each of the speeches that follow would take about five minutes to deliver. Don't make the mistake of starting your speech at one o'clock *sharp* and finishing at two o'clock *dull*.

SAMPLE SPEECH 1

Hi, my name's John and I'm an alcoholic. Ooops, sorry, that's Wednesday nights!

On behalf of all the attendants I'd like to thank Alan sincereley for those generous words. I haven't been as nervous as this since the last time I went to the clap clinic, so I prepared a few lines – and having sorted them, I feel absolutely fine. I knew it would be very difficult to follow Alan's speech ... and I was right – I couldn't follow a word of it.

Someone once said being asked to be the best man is like being asked to sleep with the Queen – it's a great honour to be asked, but nobody really wants to do it. Anyway, the Queen is at Balmoral today, so here I am. Actually, it's great being here, because after all the years I've known him, Alan has finally admitted that I am the best man.

As the best man, I have had to ensure that the groom arrives on time, sober ... and smart. Well, two out of three isn't bad. After all look what I have had to work with. I'm the best man – not a magician.

So, starting from the beginning, Alan was born at a very early age. He was born in Birmingham on the 18th January 1968. He was so surprised by his birth that he was speechless for about a year and a half. Actually his mum tells me he came prematurely – so nothing new there then, eh Jill? I'm not saying he was ugly, but his mum told me she used to have to put a bone round his neck, so the dog would play with him.

I asked his dad if he had any cute photos of Alan that I could show today. There was this really sweet one of him lying naked on a sheepskin rug playing with his little organ ... he's always been a very musical chap ... I was going to have it blown up to show you today, but then I thought it might be too embarrassing because it was only taken last year.

Alan grew up eventually and attended various schools around the country. I am told he was an ideal pupil, who excelled in most subjects. Sorry that should have read: 'he was an idle pupil, who was expelled from most subjects.' In fact last week whilst at home in Coventry I dug out his last report. Mr Martin, the Head said, and I quote. . . . 'I am convinced that Alan will go far, and the sooner he's far away from us the better. . . .'. And so he took that advice literally and moved to London.

Anyway moving swiftly on. The happy couple. Jill looks absolutely stunning today. Alan looks stunned. No seriously, you've scrubbed up quite nicely and you look very smart. They certainly knew how to make suits back in the nineteen eighties, didn't they? Isn't it funny how history repeats itself. Only 27 years ago Jill's parents were sending her to bed with a dummy – and tonight there'll be Alan.

Everybody here knows Alan in a different way. He's a loving son, a friend, a confidante – an all round pain in the arse. I have also known many actually compare him to God. They note that he's rarely seen, is holier than thou and if he does any work it's a miracle.

Before I make the toast, I have a few words of wisdom I'd like to pass on.
To Alan:
Any man who thinks he is smarter than his wife is married to a very smart woman.
To Jill:
If you love something, set it free,
If it comes back, it was, and always will be, yours,
If it never returns, it was never yours to begin with,
If it just sits in your room, messes up your stuff, eats your food, uses the telephone, takes your money, and never behaves as if you set it free in the first place, you either married it or gave birth to it.

You know, this really is a truly historic day! This day, the 21st July, will always be associated with three of the great events of the last hundred years. Funnyman Robin Williams was born in 1952; Neil Armstrong took a giant leap for mankind in 1969; and on this day in 200X, Alan married Jill! So in 1969 it was Neil Armstrong, but today it is Alan who is over the moon.

Please everyone join me in toasting the health and happiness of the bride and groom – Alan and Jill!

Now I believe there have been one or two cards and e-mails . . .

SAMPLE SPEECH 2

Good afternoon. I'm known as Dave Can I Get You Another Drink? I'd love to talk to as many of you as possible later. I'll be at the bar. Please address me by my full name.

On behalf of Sarah and me, thanks very much Mike, for those kind words. Can I just say, Sarah – you look fantastic and you've done a great job getting Anne here in one piece and keeping her quiet for long enough for Mike to make his vows. Mike, I think your speech was the most I've heard you say over the last couple of years without mentioning football.

You might be interested to know, as members of his band will testify, he often suffers from nerves before a performance, and he confided in me earlier today that he was feeling pretty nervous. The problem is Mike's nerves play havoc with his bowels – put it this way, when he gave his speech, it wasn't the first time today he's got up from a warm seat with a piece of paper in his hand.

I must say I was very happy when Mike called me a few

months ago to say he had finally asked Anne to marry him. I was honoured when he asked me to be his best man, so I'd like to thank Anne for telling him to choose me. I was also very excited about the prospect of being able to talk for longer than ten seconds, without her interrupting.

Anyway, I've taken my duties as best man pretty seriously. One of the first things I did was to buy a couple of books to read to get a better idea of my responsibilities and I'd like to share a few of these with you. I think I've succeeded in my first duty today, which was to get Mike here, firstly on time . . . a rarity, secondly . . . sober . . . unusual, and thirdly, smart . . . which is unheard of.

Of course, we all know that these days, one of the main responsibilities of the best man is to organise the stag weekend. Now Mike's a classy kind of guy, so I thought the stag weekend should take place somewhere appropriate. I thought about Mike's career in the City, and considered one of the major financial capitals of the world like Tokyo, New York or Frankfurt. Then I thought about his good looks and superb dress sense and thought perhaps a city renowned for it's style, like Paris or Milan. In the end, I realised there was a town right here in the UK that reflects Mike's personality perfectly. So we went to West Hartlepool.

We found a good nightclub and had a quiet drink. Until then I hadn't realised that it only takes one drink to get Mike drunk . . . the tenth. Anyway, Mike couldn't find the toilet, so he said to the barmaid, 'I'm desperate to spend a penny.' And she replied, 'You're showing your age, love. We're European now . . . people don't "spend a penny" anymore . . . they Euro-nate!'

Our hero had his trousers removed and was tied to some railings in front of the nightclub at chucking out time. Don't worry – there wasn't much to see. Small but perfectly formed. He has asked me to mention that it was bloody cold that night.

As Max Bygraves used to say, I wanna tell you a story, because I think it sums up the kind of man Anne has married. Soon after we met, Mike invited me to his eighteenth birthday party. At the time I hardly knew anyone in Manchester – in fact I was getting a bit depressed with life. Mike didn't really know me that well, either – I was an acquaintance of a friend of a friend. But despite this he absolutely insisted I came to his do. He wouldn't take no for an answer and he almost forced details of his address upon me. For the first time since I moved there, I felt wanted.

He said, 'A number 23 bus will bring you right to my door – 9 Rosamond Street. Walk up to the front door and press the doorbell with your elbow.' 'Why my elbow, Mike?' I asked. 'Because you'll have a bottle of wine under one arm, a box of chocolates under the other, a four-pack in one hand and my pressie in the other, won't you?' he replied. Yes, Anne, that's the kind of man you've married.

Anne, I can't understand why you chose Mike rather than me. But I suppose it proves men have better taste than women. After all, Mike chose Anne, but Anne chose Mike. Mike there's nothing I wouldn't do for you, and I know there's nothing you wouldn't do for me. In fact, we spend our lives doing nothing for each other.

Seriously though, Mike, you are a very lucky man to have married Anne – but then again Anne, you are an equally lucky lady to have married Mike, and on behalf of the bridesmaids, I wish you both love and happiness. Ladies and Gentlemen, a toast: to the new Mr and Mrs Giles: to Mike and Anne!

SAMPLE SPEECH 3

Ladies and Gentlemen and those of neither status, I shall not be speaking for long because of my throat. If I go on too long Liz has threatened to cut it.

You know, when Steve first asked me to be his best man ... organise the stag party, make sure he got to the church on time, say a few nice words about him at the reception ... I told him he might be better off with someone else, seeing as I live 200 miles away now. But then Steve turned around and offered me twenty quid. I couldn't believe it, and I told him in no uncertain terms that I'm a man of principle and can't be bought. I was also a little insulted that he thought twenty quid could buy my friendship ... then he upped his offer to fifty quid ... so here I am!

I have not taken my responsibilities as best man lightly. I have done my homework and found that there are three essential elements of a wedding day and they are as follows:

The Aisle – it's the longest walk you'll ever take;
The Alter – the place where two become one;
The Hymn – the celebration of marriage.

I think Wendy must have read the same book because as she took her place beside Steve today, I swear I heard her whisper: Aisle Altar Hymn . . . Aisle Altar Hymn. Steve, you have been warned!

Thank you, Steve for those kind words about the bridesmaids. Personally, though, I would have gone further. They are the most delightful set of bridesmaids I have ever seen. Be honest, today you are blinkered and you only have eyes for Wendy – and who can blame you?

Let me begin by putting Steve out of his misery. There are some stories you can tell at a wedding and then there are others that might be interesting, but can't really be told. The ones Steve made up about himself for the Readers' Letters section of *Men Only* would be an example.

I won't mention the special name his mum had for him. I won't mention what Little Willy, sorry what Steve did, that scandalised his neighbours, and whatever he's done with rubber chickens in the past . . . well, that's his own business. That's not the aspect of his life I want to talk about today, not among such nice company.

What can I tell you about Steve that hasn't already been said on *Neighbours From Hell* and on *Crimewatch UK*? As you all know, he has a great sense of humour. I will give you an example of what he might say to the hotel room service lady in the morning after the wedding night. Steve will call down to their hotel room service and order breakfast. For himself he'll order a full English with two eggs, and a pint of orange juice. For his new wife, he'll order a piece of lettuce and a carrot. The room service lady will of course be puzzled by this request, and ask him whether Mrs Jones might want something more substantial, to which Steve will probably reply, 'I'm conducting an experiment to see if she eats like a rabbit as well.'

Steve tells me he expects the honeymoon to be like a good chicken dinner: a lot of breast, a little bit of leg, and a lot of stuffing. Or perhaps like a table: four bare legs and no drawers. He thinks that the honeymoon should not go on for longer than five days or he'll get a weak end.

Behind his demeanour, he is however, a gentle and considerate person. So, Wendy, you must promise me to be good to Steve, treat him with loving care and affection, or even better, treat him like a flower – grab him by the stalk.

All joking aside, Steve, you're a great guy and an excellent friend; I'll never forget the favours you've done for me, and the good times we've had. Thanks for giving me the opportunity, privilege and honour of standing here today, by being your best man. Wendy, you make a beautiful wife, and I am very confident that you'll make each other very happy. Let me just say that from my perspective Wendy couldn't be marrying a better man, and Steve couldn't be marrying a better woman, and I am extremely happy to have you both as friends.

Before I make the toast, I would like to share this parting thought with you all: Steve is no Einstein and Wendy is always on a diet. And that's why they are sure to stick together, through thick and thin.

Ladies and Gentlemen, on behalf of the bridesmaids and myself I'd like you all to raise your glasses to toast Mr & Mrs Jones . . . to Little Willy and . . . I mean to Steve and Wendy. Congratulations. We all wish you all the very best for the future!

A FINAL WORD

Well all good things must come to an end . . . and so must this book! Now it's over to you. You know the ground rules, so just relax and have fun. In the words of the famous song penned by the only Oscar to have won an Oscar – Oscar Hammerstein – I wish you 'Happy Talk'!